I Can Get Dressed

Written by Chemise Taylor

Illustrated by Alexis B. Taylor

Copyright © 2019 by My Skills Books

Published by My Skills Books

All rights reserved. No part of this publication may be reproduced, distributed, or transmitted in any form or by any means, including photocopying, recording, or other electronic or mechanical methods, without the prior written permission of the publisher, except in the case of brief quotations embodied in critical reviews and certain other noncommercial uses permitted by copyright law.

First Printing, 2019.

ISBN: 978-1-951573-09-6

www.myskillsbooks.com

Mom says, "Are you wearing that today?

"We are going to see a play. Go and get changed right away."

Hmmm. What should I choose?

I've got the perfect outfit right here!

First, I take off my old clothes.

Now, I can put on the outfit I chose.

I start with my favorite red skirt.

It goes well with this fun shirt.

I put on my long, comfy socks.

I put on my pink shoes. I like them a lot.

Last but not least, I put on my bright, red beret.

I'm all dressed! I'm ready to have a fun day.

Book Details

Story Word Count: 101

Key Words: Get, Dressed, Put, On, Socks, Skirt, Shirt, Shoes, Hat

Comprehension Check
- What was the story about?
- Where is she going?
- What did she put on?

Reading Award

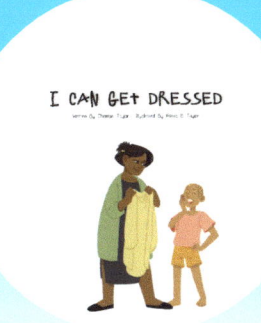

This certificate goes to:

_____

for reading "I Can Get Dressed"

Good Job!

More books, apps and resources at myskillsbooks.com

www.ingramcontent.com/pod-product-compliance
Lightning Source LLC
Chambersburg PA
CBHW042108090526

44591CB00004B/51